To Amy
Love from Alison
Xmas '87

Amy .L

GW00504190

Jill Waterman

Harry's Sizes

Burke Books ▶◀ LONDON * TORONTO * NEW YORK

First published 1985
Reprinted 1985
© Jill Waterman 1985

CIP data
Waterman, Jill E.
Harry's sizes.
I. Title
823'.914 [J]   PZ7
ISBN 0 222 01042 8

Burke Publishing Company Limited
Pegasus House, 116-120 Golden Lane, London EC1Y 0TL, England.
Burke Publishing (Canada) Limited
Registered Office: 20 Queen Street West, Suite 3000, Box 30,
Toronto, Canada M5H 1V5.
Burke Publishing Company Inc.
Registered Office: 333 State Street, PO Box 1740,
Bridgeport, Connecticut 06601, U.S.A.
Filmset by Graphiti (Hull) Ltd., Hull, England.
Printed in The Netherlands by Deltaprint Holland.

This is Harry.
He is going somewhere special today.

Here are Harry's Mummy and Daddy.
They are going somewhere special too.

This is Harry's sister. Her name is Daisy.
She is going with them.

fat

thin

They are all going to a wildlife park.
Harry is taking his fat teddy-bear
and Daisy is taking her thin doll.

tall

short

Now they are
ready to get on the bus.
Look at tall Daddy
beside short Daisy.

wide

narrow

Now they have arrived at the park.
There are two ways to go in:
a wide road for buses and cars
and a narrow path for people.

enormous

teeny

"Oh! Look at that enormous elephant,"
shouts Harry.
Daisy likes the teeny ladybird better.

deep

shallow

Here are the polar bears and penguins.
"The polar bears' water is very deep,
but the penguins' pool is only shallow,"
Daddy tells them.

huge

tiny

Now they are looking at the gorillas,
Can *you* see the tiny baby
in the arms of its huge mother?

large

small

Daddy, Mummy, Harry and
Daisy are eating ice-cream.
Three of them have small cones,
but one has a large cone!
Can *you* guess who that is?

high

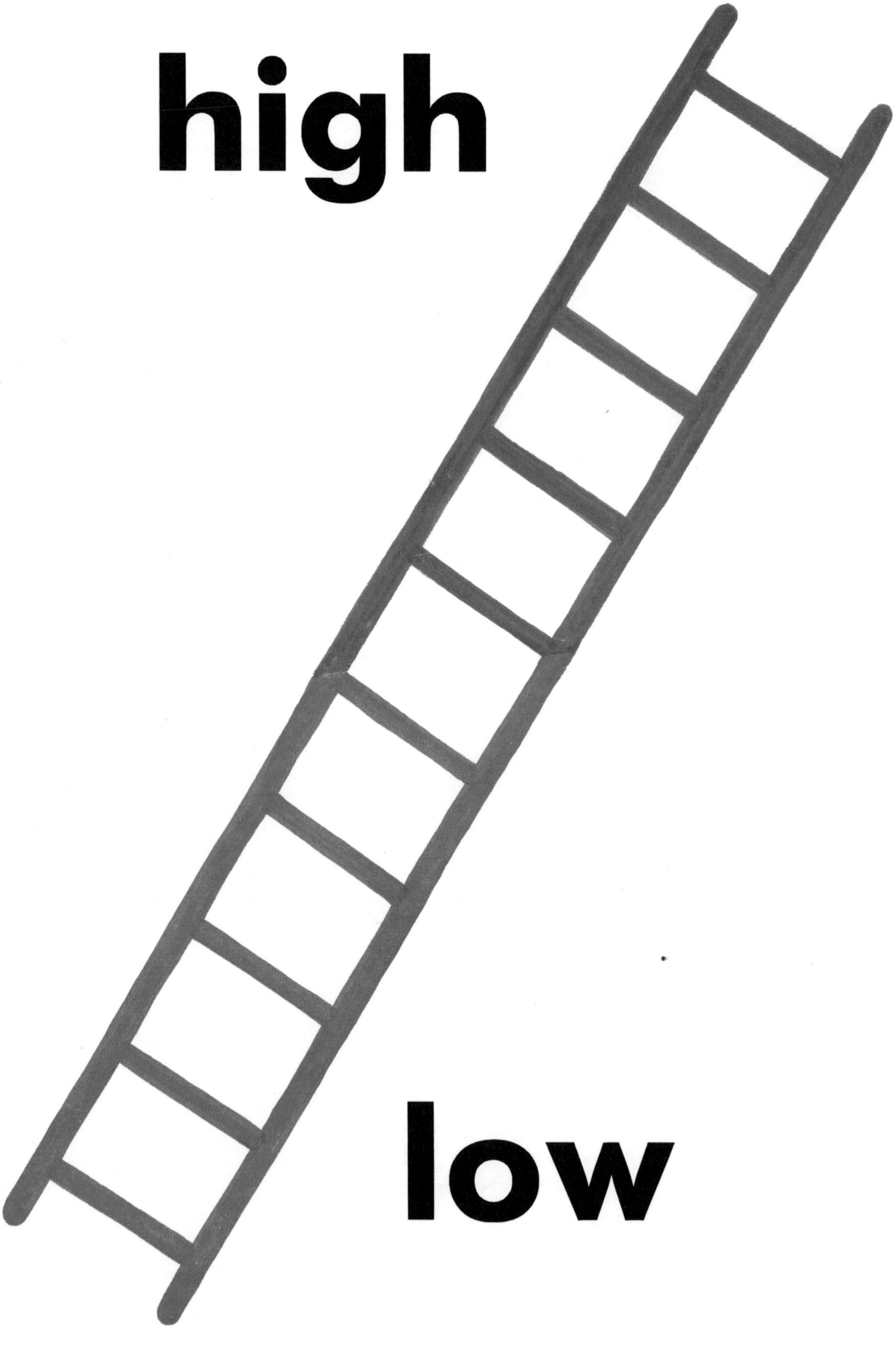

low

Here they are in the play area.
Look! Harry is down low on the slide
and Daisy is up high.
Hold tight, Daisy!

long

short

Now they are looking at the crocodiles.
"Look!" says Harry,
"The mother crocodile is very long
and the babies are very short."

big

little

Here they are with the fish.
"They are all different sizes," says Harry.
"Some are big, some are little
and some are in between."

Now it is time to go home.
Daisy is very tired. She is such a little girl
and she has walked a long, long way.

They have only a short walk to the bus.
"I'm going to take huge strides," says Harry,
"so that I'll be there first!"

On the bus, Daddy says, "Look at those tall trees,
they were tiny seeds once;
but some things get smaller, like your pencils
— the more you use them the smaller they get!"

"Some things always stay the same size,"
says Mummy. "Your shoes never grow,
but your feet do!"

When they reach home, Harry says,
"I'm going to look at the sizes of all our toys.
Some are large, and some are small.
Some are fat and some are thin.
Some are short and some are tall."

Can *you* see lots of different sizes around you?

Harry and Daisy are ready for bed now.
What a long day they have had.
Goodnight Harry! Goodnight Daisy! Sleep well!